Dialect of a Skirt

Dialect of a Skirt

Erica Miriam Fabri

Hanging Loose Press
Brooklyn, New York

Copyright © 2010 by Erica Miriam Fabri

Published by Hanging Loose Press, 231 Wyckoff Street, Brooklyn, New York 11217. All Rights Reserved. No part of this book may be reproduced without the publisher's written permission, except for brief quotations in reviews.

www.hangingloosepress.com

Printed in the United States of America
10 9 8 7 6 5 4 3 2 1

Hanging Loose Press thanks the Literature Program of the New York State Council on the Arts for a grant in support of the publication of this book.

Cover design by Black Cracker

Cover and Author Photographs: Linda Turley

Acknowledgments: Page 87

Library of Congress Cataloging-in-Publication Data

Fabri, Erica Miriam
  Dialect of a skirt / Erica Miriam Fabri.
    p. cm.
Poems.
ISBN 978-1-934909-10-2 (pbk.)
I. Title.
PS3606.A245D53 2010
811'.6--dc22
                                    2009034947

Produced at The Print Center, Inc. 225 Varick St., New York, NY 10014, a non-profit facility for literary and arts-related publications. (212) 206-8465

Contents

Dear Poetry Editor, Please Publish My Poems 9

1. The Pencil Skirt

Dialect of a Skirt 13
Socks and Swimsuits 14
In Jacklight 15
The Corpse Dream 16
Biracial Marriage 17
The Word-Lover's Miscarriage 18
Sappho on the Lower East Side 19
The Waitress 20
The Poet and the Muse 21
When the Muse Comes Home 22
The Secret Language of Symbols 23

2. The Garter Belt

Marilyn and the Spelling Bee 27
"Marilyn Monroe was born with a diamond stud in her nose" 28
"When Marilyn Monroe made love to Joan Crawford" 29
The Third Miscarriage of Marilyn Monroe 30
Sylvia and Marilyn in the Land of Milk and Honey 31
Betsey Johnson at the Murray Hill Medical Center 32
Lucky Bee 33
Mannequins at Lunch 35
The First Plastic Surgery Patient on Earth 36
Hijab 38
Pocket Wife 39

3. The Corset

Grandmother Love Poem 43
Fishwife 44

Stealing the Baby	45
How to Make a "Virgin"	46
The Nightgown	47
Christmas Poem	50
Dear Lion,	52
Dear Girl,	53

4. The Miniskirt

The Monster	57
Blessing	58
The Poet and Her True Love	59
Fairy Tale	60
My Funny Valentine	61
The Poet and the Truck Driver	62
The Art of Compromise	63
The Poet and the Egyptian	64
Bangladesh	65
Hip-Hop in the Desert	66
Holy Is the Secular World	67
"When I fell in love with the leper"	68

5. The Silk Shop

The String	71
The Doppelganger Love Poem	72
"He said: you are a white elephant,"	73
Trading Pigs for Love	74
Love in an Ice Cream Truck	76
The Smallest Bird on Earth	78
Twenty-Four Hours	79
"The last time they made love"	81
The Snake Who Swallows His Own Tail	82
The Eye Is an Organ of Light	83
Where the Good Men Live	84
The Animal of Love	86

*For my grandmother,
who knew I was a poet
even before I knew it myself.*

Dear Poetry Editor, Please Publish My Poems

I will be frank: I want to become a poet
while I am still young and rare.
I want to be a foxy poet.

I am aware that in the old Welsh tradition
one must apprentice to a master for nine years
before becoming a poet.

I will be frank: This is not Wales.
New York is a full-feathered, fat city.
One year has the rag trade of a lifetime.

I do not have nine lives to spare.
Dear Editor, this is what I have
to offer you: a bathtub full of moon

rocks, a whole Central Station of sacred
mules, and all the wild groceries of a French
circus. It is a sharp tooth that I am submitting

for your review. It is a Monster.
I will be frank: If this is not enough,
I don't know what is.

1. The Pencil Skirt

Dialect of a Skirt

The young girl wanted a new voice. After all, people got
new things every day. A new hip, a new nose, a new set
of suspenders. She adored the consonants that landed
like wooden shoes. She loved the type of L-sounds
that made a mouth drool from the back of the tongue
to the front. She practiced her new voice into seashells,
tin cans, caves. She gave her first performance quietly,
into the ear of her sleeping dog. She could tell by his snorting
that his dreams were of fat tree trunks and black, truffle-filled
soil. Later, she drove to the local gas station and used her new
voice to ask for a pack of cigarettes. She wasn't wearing a bra,
but the attendant didn't notice. He was too busy *listening*
to the way sound seemed to drip out of her mouth,
as she said the word *Camel*.

Socks and Swimsuits

The boy said, The only way to prove that our friendship is true is to swim naked together.
The girl said, Okay, but for each sock we take off, we'll tell one secret.

The boy said, Okay. Left sock, have you ever masturbated?
The girl said, Yeah. Left sock, how many times a day do you get a boner?

The boy said, Eight or nine times. Right sock, what do you use to masturbate?
The girl said, My finger. Right sock, what makes you get a boner?

The boy said, That's easy. Asses, boobs, legs, when a girl licks her lips, and warm water.
The girl said, To get my bathing suit off you've got to tell me something really secret that I never would have guessed and it has to be true.

The boy said, Okay. I only have one ball.
The girl said, No way.

The boy said, I swear, you can ask my mom.
The girl said, No way am I going to ask your mom.

The boy said, Now you've got to tell me something.
The girl said, Okay, me and Janie got naked and practiced humping.

The boy said nothing.
The girl said, I swear, you can ask Janie.

The boy said nothing.
The girl turned her back to him and slid out of her bathing suit. She jumped off the dock into the water.

The boy slid off his swim shorts and dove in, head first.

In Jacklight

What are you doing? he asked, when he felt one finger
and one lip touch his chin: *looking for words*, she said.
How many have you found so far? he wanted to know,
because he had heard a bag of wooden letters rattle in the dark.
Thirteen, she told him. *What do they say?* he pressed his ear
to her mouth. She went like this:

lean on the concrete ledge. smoke hard, with dog-neck in your fist.

Ooo, he said, *I like them*, and a shine swung by, for just a stint, as if
they were sleeping bull's-eye to a lighthouse. In jacklight,
she could see he was smiling, his grin was a glass bowl.
She reached her finger out again, and her lip. *No*, he said, *before
you go and find new ones, tell me those again, in another way.*
She said, *okay, here's this:*

hard dog, smoke the concrete with your fist on. ledge, lean neck-in.

The Corpse Dream

For three days now, she has not been able to erase her dream:
She is locked in a basement. Dead bodies are laid out on rows of folding tables.
Her great aunt Kuku is back from the grave to count the crumbled souls.
Kuku carries a red candle, stops at each cold figure and pins a yellow ticket
to their shirts. The ticket says: **PASSPORT TO HELL**.

In the morning, she wakes her American boyfriend and says to him: *I need you
to hear what I saw, so that I can forget it.* Her nickname for him is *Boobs*.
She whispers: *Boobs, there were corpses.* He sticks his thumbs inside his ears, refuses
to hear a word of it. That night, she tries again: *Boobs, I need you to hear what I saw.
Boobs, there were corpses.* He covers her mouth with a sock.

The corpse dream follows her like a swarm of bees. In the dark, she can hear Kuku
counting in Chinese. At the bus stop, she sees a yellow ticket nailed
to a wall. She wears her hair in a soft French crop: on the third night, she lays it
on their pillow like a quiet blackbird and begs him: *Please listen. Boobs,
there were corpses…*

Biracial Marriage

for K-Swift

He wanted her to make a greenhouse of her body, so he bought her a book about carrots.
Read to her, from chapter two, where ancient Greeks used the root vegetable
as a love medicine, and gentlemen in Tehran boiled them in sugar.
He said, *Tonight, let's make a stew.*

But she was afraid that, if they made a son, her father would never hold him
without wearing gloves. Or if they knocked together a daughter, his mother
would refuse to braid her curls.

After dinner, he left a torn-out page from chapter four next to her perfume,
where it explained how carrots actually exist in a rainbow of colors: *purple-skinned,
white-fleshed, red and yellow*—and that in fact, the deep-sweet orange
that we know today is actually the love-child of a pale yellow and a dark red.

At midnight, she let him climb through her like a weed. Her arms and legs let go of her,
rippled like worms in sun. He opened the window to let in the moon, then wrapped
a lock of her hair around his ear like a vine.

That night, she dreamt of a baby born with the skin of a giraffe. And twins that did not
share the same kind of lips. She woke in a cold sweat and opened the carrot book
to chapter six, read how a woman can eat the seeds after love-making, to make her
slippery inside, so that a child can slide out from her legs before it even begins to grow.

She untied her hair and crept out onto the fire escape. Their vegetable garden was an old
plastic crate. She got on her knees in the stark white light and began to dig deep
into the box of wet soil. She closed her eyes and used the tips of her fingers
to search the dirt for seeds.

The Word-Lover's Miscarriage

Something[1] about[2] the[3] word[4] *Chelsea*[5], it's[6] almost[7] as[8] charming[9] as[10] *notch*[11].

---

[1] **Something: 1.** the opposing noun to anything or nothing **2.** first word in the song "Something in the Way She Moves" by the Beatles, the song he used to sing to her when she locked herself in the bathroom **3.** the only way to get her out

[2] **about: 1.** when he is never calling or never stopping over or never driving by, he is in colloquial terms "not about" **2.** when he is in her room or in her bed or in the toilet or in the kitchen or wandering into broom closets, he is in colloquial terms "about"

[3] **the: 1.** word-parasite that gives an object, thing or person a quality of Godliness and Superiority; example #1: *a* turtle (common), *the* turtle (blue-blooded), example #2: *a* fucking bitch (any woman), *the* fucking bitch (her)

[4] **word: 1.** sounds that poets use to make music **2.** letters of the alphabet when they've formed clubs **3.** what he hasn't uttered to her in three years

[5] **Chelsea: 1.** neighborhood in the borough of Manhattan where they lived together **2.** girl's name deriving from an ancient frog myth **3.** Aeslehc printed backwards **4.** the name of a girl she knew in Girl Scout camp who was sent home early with her period (there was blood *everywhere!*)

[6] **it's:** contraction made of two words—[it] and [is]—most often used when he is very drunk and his tongue is too sloppy to say the words separately

[7] **almost: 1.** a very small measurement of time or space **2.** how close he came that night to killing her with an awl

[8] **as:** the word used to differentiate the two men he was; example: *as* a sober man he was her lover; but *as* a drunk he was a boxer beating her like a rake, turning her pink skin a mottled red and blue

[9] **charming:** what he was *not* when he stood on her stomach, kicked with his heels and cursed

[10] **as:** also used to differentiate the difference in size between two people; example: he weighed twice *as* much *as* she did

[11] **notch: 1.** the single-syllable word she chose to name the scar just below her belt where he cut her open **2.** her favorite word; she works it into every one of her poems

Sappho on the Lower East Side

She works in a tattoo parlor. Her shop
is small and dark, just like her women.
Young girls come all the way
from New Jersey to find her.

She will only tattoo two things:
a crocus in full bloom
or the word *Helen*.

She will only tattoo in one place:
the nape of the neck.

The girls are lined up for twenty blocks,
in vinyl skirts or paper-thin
eyelet dresses—they are waiting their turn

to lift the hair from their shoulders
and say: *Sappho, give me your needle*.

The Waitress

I was the "section one" girl, and she was seated in "section two"
when she flagged me down. Her coffee sat in front of her
like a frog. *I need to tell you exactly how it happened*,
she said, tilting her hand at the mug as if it were an exhibit.
*I asked the other waitress if the coffee was fresh, and she
looked into my eyes and told me, yes.* I said nothing.
There was nothing to say. She continued: *It's ice cold,
and thick as mud*. Before I could apologize she repeated, hard:
She looked into my eyes and told me, yes. I noticed small gray
hairs curling around her ear and thin lines like wires above her lip.
Surely—she was older than me—this cannot have been the first time
she had trusted someone, and been deceived. We both looked down
at the deep, dark liquid. I decided not to make any excuses.
I'll make you a new pot, I told her, *I promise*.

The Poet and the Muse

He said: How many poems have you written for me?
She said: One for every rabbit in the cemetery.

He said: How many names do I have?
She said: One for every mailbox on our road.

He said: Can you erase birthmarks?
She said: Skin stains the page.

He said: Can I kick down a tree?
She said: Flat feet always make wood sounds.

He said: Do we marry?
She said: A thousand times.

He said: Babies?
She said: They've grown. Stubborn and reckless.

He said: Do I become an old man?
She said: You wrench me out of our bed.

He said: Am I better in stanza than in flesh?
She said: I forget. Remind me again how muscle tastes.

When the Muse Comes Home

When the Muse comes home he wants to know where supper is.
He knows you've cracked all the eggs and used the shells for a mural.
He wants to have his flannel shirts folded, and he knows you pet them,
with one eye closed—trying to find the right metaphor for lamb's belly.
He is glowing blue, like he was in last week's poem, but he is still hungry
and horny—and he is solid—he can be touched!—different from the sonnet

where your hand slid through his liver—(as if he was made of fog or jelly!)—
and he is annoyed that you think *work* is this: imagining him
in different-shaped hats, spending hours thinking up new ways to say *red*,
rearranging words that you find on his shampoo bottle
to make one couplet that says with pinwheel precision what it's like
to have the Muse sleeping under your yellow arm:

It is the *openhanded fullness of strawberry juice.*
The *fresh silk of freshly-picked hair.*

The Secret Language of Symbols

What if I say you are the man who wears fish
for shoes, or that you hide beneath a girl's green
dress? What if I tell them I found you inside a bottle
or a lamp, and that in there, you were holding
a small brown bird under your tongue? What if
I write this on snakeskin: *Deep inside his eye sockets
there are jellyfish.* You told me you came from a place
where stampedes of horses hunt in the valley of your ribcage.
I told you that's where I came from, too. *Funny, I never
saw you there*, you said. *Yes you did. I was the one
selling ice tea from inside a cardboard box.* What if
the pills you swallow are actually dragonflies, rubbing
the dust from their wings all over your belly? What if
there is an octopus in your backyard? What if there are
firecrackers in your onions? What if I spray-paint
a secret message on the curved wall of a drain tunnel
that when deciphered means: *His body was a drum
and his hands were horns. He made a song that turned
my throat into a wishing well and filled me with pennies
that flickered like copper stars.*

2. The Garter Belt

Marilyn and the Spelling Bee

It was an early round.
The judge presented it to her: *Fish*.
The pride knife stabbed at her:
SPELL IT, NORMA.

She *knew* she knew this one.
As she dug her two beautiful
bucked teeth
into her too beautiful
bottom lip
and started
to say: *eff*—
two droplets
of nearly black blood
ran down her clefted chin.

Just then: Agatha.

Agatha, breastless, wanted to win.
Agatha said: *Blood isn't allowed*
      in a Spelling Bee.
         Sit down, Norma Jean.

Agatha pressed
the bridge of her glasses
into her forehead,
hard, like bone.

Marilyn Monroe was born with a diamond stud in her nose

but the Big Bitch at Blue Book Modeling made her take it out.
She yanked it straight, and a bump of blood
went like drool over her beauty mark.

She didn't know what to do with it
so she placed it on her tongue like a pill,
and gulped it down.

Norma in the mirror said:
"How can you do it, Girl?
Just take it like that?"

"Silly Jeanie," Marilyn told her:
"I've swallowed far worse—
try a fat pearl, that's wretched!"

In 1948, an old orthodontist named Walter
fixed her "one bad tooth."

She packed a carpetbag full of Tru-Glo make-up
and moved into the Beverly Hills Hotel.

Then, Johnny Hyde made an appointment
to have her hairline raised with electrolysis,
to cut the bone of her nose, to shoot silicone
into her chin, and to remove the extra toe
from her left foot.

After that, Marilyn never closed her mouth again.

"This is monkey business," she was telling her reflection,
when Truman Capote found her sitting for hours,
staring into a looking glass,
"What are you doing, Marilyn?" he asked.
 "Just looking at her," she said.

When Marilyn Monroe made love to Joan Crawford

she used her one webbed foot,
shaped like a bat's wing,
to part Joan's hair in five places.

The Third Miscarriage of Marilyn Monroe

There was blood on the backside of her white sharkskin dress
cramping a cutthroat charley horse.
Doctor Krohn said:
*I warned her she would kill a baby
with the drink and the pills,*

Johnnie the driver slapdashed her to Cedars of Lebanon;
she filled the ER with the stink of Chanel No. 5 and hemoglobin.

Another bucket of plasma, slosh, for the wastebasket,
no daughter, with a sixth toe like Mom, to borrow the hand-trimmed
nylon eyelashes, or to have raw-liver juice at breakfast
and BIG POTS of caviar at lunch.

She asked for an injection of Mickey Finn knockout drops:
like a sharpshooter Doc popped her with a chloral hydrate enema.
She closed her cornflower-blue eyes, and her face went slack
as if she died between wolf calls.

Sylvia and Marilyn in the Land of Milk and Honey

Their afterlife would surely look like New York City.
When Sylvia walks, her red high heels
stab the sidewalk. Marilyn doesn't wear shoes. In fact,
she doesn't wear anything except her platinum bob.
They go to a drag queen named Bambi to buy their
favorite shades of blonde in a bottle. Sylvia always gets
Creamsicle. Marilyn prefers *Pale Champagne*. They help
each other rub the bleach into their roots and wrap
their heads in tinfoil. Sylvia sets an egg timer for nine years
and sits down to write a sonnet. She asks Marilyn to give her
two words. Marilyn says, *White piano*, and pulls up a bathtub
to rest in. There is no sun here, nor any kind of night, but they
don't mind much. So long as they have lipstick and ink.
The timer goes *tick, tick, tick…*

Betsey Johnson at the Murray Hill Medical Center

"It was all very spaceship," she told the receptionist
who asked about her days with the Velvet Underground.
At Christmas, she made sweaters for the nurses,
with brightly-colored fish or skulls sewn into the wool.
For checkups, she always wore a dress made of cellophane
so the doctor could see right through to her heart,
and she tied her zebra-like hair extensions
into the shape of a spider plant, to keep them
out of the way. He pressed his stethoscope against
the lightning bolt on her chest, and listened.
Betsey asked him to describe the way it looked.
"Like a deep purple evening bag, with thick
drawstrings." Then, she asked about the pumping.
"That *lub dub, lub dub* sound? Why, Ms. Johnson,
those are the tiny stars moving like rockets inside you."
Her giant red lips nodded. On her way out, she winked
at the woman from Billing, and said the same thing
she always did: "Darling, what would *you* wear on the moon?"

Lucky Bee

My mother made me wear this dress.

This costume of the bourgeois.

These bustles, hoops and frills—so heavy
a girl can't run even if a bear is chasing her.

This knot of feathers on my hat, which looks like I carry
a murder of crows on the crown of my head—it isn't the real me.

I'm going to tell you why I'm really here, and it's not
to get a photo of myself with kitchen doilies draped

over my shoulders, and the arm of a rosebush
curling around my neck like a snake.

I know what you folks do
down here at the Haymarket Theater.

I'm nineteen now, been practicing my giggle
in the bathtub for years. I know I will be

the hottest piece of something sweet
that this burlesque stage has ever seen.

I never let myself look shopworn.
I know that if you toss your garter

into the audience, you can end up arrested.
I know that being a vaudeville doll

isn't as simple as keeping
your pasties sparkly,

and I know that a girl can't get by
on sequins or tassels alone.

I won't use any old-hat stunts or monkeyshine—
like the others do—no fire-breathing, no duck-tricks—

instead, I've got a secret move
that no chorus girl on earth can beat:

at the end of my routine, I reach
into my panties and pull a live mouse

from my peach. I hold it by its tail
to show the front row how it squeaks,

then swallow it down
like a gumdrop.

Mannequins at Lunch

Two mannequins sit at a table together in a fancy restaurant.
They are drinking wine the color of blood.

One pulls a shoe out of her handbag;
she uses the pointy heel to open a cockle-shell.

The other cries into her soup.
When her teardrops land in the broth they sound like metal.

An Indian woman gets up from her booth and approaches them.
She asks politely: *What is it like to see everything through such a hard face?*

The first mannequin says: *It is constant vertigo.*
Then the second one adds: *Yes. It's like worms on the shower curtain,*
    when you're just trying to get clean.

The First Plastic Surgery Patient on Earth

I see your beauty. I hear your need.
—Mahatma Gandhi

No one knows her name. Only that she hated her face
in the same way a witch hates water.

She found Sushruta on the banks of the Ganges.
He was practicing his surgeries on watermelons,
clay pots and reeds. He promised her beauty, if only
she would believe in his art.

Sushruta, nimble and vigilant, shaved off
his beard, cut his nails. Fed her wine and gingerly
trimmed some flesh from her forehead, some skin
from her chin. Then, he worked her mask
like bread dough, to reshape
the unshapely places.

He didn't tell her that it would take time to heal.
Forgot to mention how she would be hideous
for weeks to come, but that eventually the two skins
would synchronize, and one day her pout
would be as polished as a lemon.

She disappeared. Didn't even leave her hair behind.

Little did she know that Sushruta would become
"The Father of Surgery," that he would go on
to reconstruct noses that had been amputated
as punishment for crimes.

That his technique would be practiced,
nearly unchanged, to this day.

Now, a woman can buy herself an upper lip,
she can have the ugly sucked right out of her with a straw.

He could have given her mangoes for breasts.
The ankles of peacocks.
The cheekbones of the Goddess Lakshmi.

Some say she threw herself into the river.
Face first.
Some say she's swimming there still.

Hijab

for Imette St. Guillen

If a man and a woman are alone in one place,
the third person present is the devil.
—attributed to the Prophet Mohammed*

Maybe we are too hard on them. The men of Islam.
Perhaps they realize the beauty of a woman better
than any other race of men.

The pearl of a fingernail grown too long,
a set of eyelashes painted black,
a cheek tinted pink with rouge—
these small ornaments,
they understand, are enough
to drive a man wild—

forget about the glory
of a whole head of curls,
the luscious jacket of skin
that covers our bones,
the soft bell of a shoulder,
the apparatus that is an ankle.

In the American papers,
a young girl is taken from a bar,
raped, cut up, taped up,
and left in a ditch
somewhere in Brooklyn.

I see her in black and white
newsprint: two slender wrists, chiseled
as wrenches, dimples deep as egg cartons,
and a whole cataract of silky hair—
I can just imagine what she must look like in color.

Maybe we are not giving them enough credit.
After all, woman *is* a ravishing thing.

Perhaps they are trying to protect us
from a hand that is shaped like their own.

* an Islamic *hadith*, one of the sayings traditionally ascribed to Muhammad, and later collected in written form.

Pocket Wife

It was the morning I finally told him, *I'm always going to be this small*,
his eyes did a slow rattle of disbelief. I said it harder, *I'm not getting any bigger,
ever.*

And that was it. Because, sometimes, a lover is just simply not
enough.

When he picked up his things and went, I was still naked, so I slipped
into a pillowcase.

It made a fine dress. I posed in the mirror like a scarecrow, pretended to have
matchsticks for fingers.

*Mirror, Mirror, in the shape of a fin, can you see them? Parts that can seem thin
as pins.*

3. The Corset

Grandmother Love Poem

poem in the voice of Madelyn Dunham, Barack Obama's grandmother

I got married on prom night, to a man my mother hated.
He was from the wrong side of the tracks. And I liked it.
He loved me, despite my beaked nose, and I loved the way
he kissed my painted eyelids when we slow-danced.
We had to keep the wedding secret until after graduation.
I held the small gold ring under my tongue all day long in school.
Then, right before bed, after I said goodnight to my parents
and whispered my prayers into my cupped hands, I'd pull it
from my lips and slide it onto my finger until morning.

When our daughter was born, we gave her a boy's name.
When she was still swimming inside me, I made a wish
that she'd be a different kind of girl, that she would dream
of rare trees and winds that were unlike our own.
Be careful what you wish for.

When she brought the African man home for dinner,
I caught her reaching for his hands under the table. I was certain
they were wolves' hands he wore, wolves' hands that went inside
my girl to shape and mold a child that would be half-wolf
when he was born. She married the African man in secret,
on an island without me. There was nothing I could do.
After all, she had inherited this wolf-heart from me,
tied it to a rope and hung it from her neck. It looked like
a divine ornament. It made a noise like thunder.

Fishwife

There's a pregnant woman at the pool. I'm watching her
get dressed. Her skin is rock-white. She's shaped like soft
wood. She has horses' thighs and work boots for arms,
carries her belly in one of them, more solid than bone.

A knot of black dreadlocks rests on her neck. Two fingers
pull a brass pin, and ropes of hair fall loose to her waist.
She raises a hand to kiss her throat with her palm—it leaves a print.
When she moves, I think she is the most beautiful thing in Brooklyn.

I smile and say hello. Shy, that she might know
how I watch her, ashamed, that she might see
how plain my body is. She steps into a papery sundress,
the one she always wears, ties a leather cord around her hips.

Her sandals are flat as leaves. Her nose-ring is a silver fishhook.
I look away, and when I'm home, I curl my fingers
into rubber bands,
and sob into the toilet bowl.

Stealing the Baby

Smells like fall today, good day for shopping. I fill an oyster-shell purse
with one-dollar bills and take the 6 train to Chinatown. The children
are bright as melons and their parents look weary from a day of selling
slippers, handbags, and wristwatches. I pass eleven perfume stands,
a bodega of silk kimonos, and a pawn shop before I see her. But when I do,
I am certain she is the one for me; she has the perfection of fruit.

I know when she is older she will love lemonade, that her hair
will never curl. I scoop her up with one arm and drop the oyster
into her carriage. I walk slow until I reach the corner, then I begin to run.

She doesn't cry much, and when she does, I kiss her hard, smearing cherry-red
lipstick all over her face and neck. I promise to never make her learn piano
or French, unless she wants to. In ten years, I'll let her tattoo her hands.
I'll buy her umbrellas and gold hairpins, and whenever she finally asks me
where it was she came from, I'll say: *You came from an oyster, and you are my pearl.*

How to Make a "Virgin"

Mother said, "No boys, Maria," but I let him bend me anyway.
He snuck in through my bedroom window like a thief
and his hands were candles.

Once he was gone, I swore on the moon he wasn't real
and almost convinced myself until morning after morning,
my stomach started turning.

My belly began rising on me like bread dough.
My mother's face looked as bloodless as a potato,
and that's why I told her this:

If you had been there, you'd understand: he *felt* like an archangel—
any girl alive would agree that he'd need six hundred
wings to lift a backbone the way he did, and that when he
called me Star of the Sea it sounded like a noise come
from a throat full of trumpets—and that only the Left Hand
of God himself could unfold the inside of a stomach
and know how to put it back together again.

My stupid mother told the town
that this was God's child inside me.
I thought for sure no one would believe it.

Instead, faster than I could say *shit*, I became this fat-ass-first-class brand
of famous. Now, they're all eating bonbons and waiting for the birth
of my angel-born baby.

Mother is making me marry a man named Joe.
He is kind and good and builds birdhouses.

I haven't slept a wink in nine long months. Some days, when I am certain
that I am about to go mad, I try to turn my head all the way around
on my shoulders. I tell myself: in a few years none of this will matter,
because I am the kind of somebody that everybody will forget.

The Nightgown

I want a God who speaks louder than whispers. –Giselle Buchanan

In Brooklyn tonight, a 14-year old girl is accused of giving birth in her parents' apartment, then throwing the baby out the window and into the courtyard in the back of the building, killing her newborn son.—A.P., 2007

1. The Garden on Ralph Avenue

The papers say it was a weed-choked yard
where they found him. But the papers lie.

There were no weeds
and there was no choke.

What grew down there, three floors below
my bedroom window, were greens that looked

like feathers in certain light, then bird tails
and fish tails in different shades of overcast gray,

then strings of hair in the not-quite-absolute
dark that, here on Ralph Avenue, we call night.

The baby was born asleep. Don't listen to them
when they say otherwise. They weren't there.

There was a dim glow from a streetlamp,
because we don't really have a moon in Brooklyn,

and a tiny body, that did not pump even for a second,
came tearing out of me like a planet.

He was hard and cold. So I tossed him
into that nursery of stuff that looked like

yarn and silk. You can go ahead and say
that I don't know much, because I'm only

fourteen. But I live just two doors down
from the Fellowship Church,

and I can't believe that any God would let
an ugly garden grow here.

2. The Fishbird-Boybaby

I could hardly call it swimming,
when all I could do was turn and shift.

But swimming is the closest I can come
to describing the months and months

of darkness, and the jelly-like pool
I waited in—where each day her soft

walls seemed to get smaller.

I could hardly call it flying,
when all I did was drop, heavy as a tomato.

But flying is the closest I can come
to describing the three-story fall I took

into a bed of fish tails and feathers,
where the air was so frigid

it felt like fire.

3. Small Blood

On Sundays, the church bells
sound as if they are pounding
against our rooftop.
That's how close to God

I've raised my girl.
I brought her up
only two doorknobs away
from those stone steps.
This world is filled with angels
that are just as imperfect as men.
Do not assume
we have had no miracles
on our doorstep,
just because there was
some small blood
in our backyard.

Christmas Poem

This Christmas, I got dolled up
to make a visit to the state pen.

Spread cherry jam on my lips,
got into a pickup truck

and followed the river
for an hour uphill.

Inside, I signed up for one hundred gold coins
and waited at a coffee machine for the Lion.

It was snowing when I first saw him,
through a window the size of a book.

He wore a red jumpsuit and sucked
on a Maverick cigarette

in the corner of his mouth
as he crossed a cement path and barbed wire.

They'd cut his sideburns. Pulled
a tooth. But the cool slug

in his getalong was sharp as ever.
We shared a bag of sour candies,

a bottle of milk. He shuffled the deck.
I was dealing seven-card rummy,

counterclockwise, when the Lion
plopped his big mitt onto the table,

then nodded for me to do the same.
He'd lost half a fingernail

from the left hand, and
our thumb knuckles

knocked against each other like rocks.
Our hands were two

maple leaves on the table:
mine a tiny yellow pocket

next to his meaty glove.
He ironed it to the small of my back

when we posed for a Polaroid
in front of a Christmas tree,

and the man who took our picture
had burns on his face

that had buckled
to the shape of mud.

Dear Lion,

I want to write you a letter as beautiful as the stars.
Because I know it's been a year now since you've seen them.
But it's so hard. The stars have that big black pool of ink
behind them, and all I have is this pen.

The stars can sit very still for hours, burning to death,
without screaming or moving an inch. I can't do that.
The stars don't complain. They are never late.
They are more faithful than monks, and even quieter.

For centuries now, men have walked off cliffs,
so mesmerized by the muscle of the stars—
women have thrown
themselves into swamps or ovens from just having
glanced their way. The stars devour the universe

and wax the firmament. I want this brand of sorcery
for you. This sort of torch box—to light your basement.

Dear Girl,

Got your postcards yesterday.
The one with the moon

and the Eiffel Tower is my favorite.
I taped it to my locker.

Not sure if you're in India yet.

Haven't really been up to much.
Playing a lot of chess.

Television keeps me amused.
The other day there was this go-go girl

that reminded me so much of you,
she even had roses in her hair like you do.

I've been learning origami.
I can make birds, flowers, deer—

even a Jack-in-the-Box that really works!
It keeps me very busy. Even though, at first,

it was so frustrating. Now, my cell
is covered with paper animals.

I'll fold something for you.

I've noticed from your letters
that you have very good handwriting,

probably the nicest I've ever seen.
Write soon. I miss you.

4. The Miniskirt

The Monster

After she made love to the Monster,
she wanted to burn her hair.
Can you blame her?
He left something rotten there.
Even witch hazel
won't make her clean.

Blessing

Because even if you hurt me, lucky thing this world,
where we get to love at all.

Because your jinx can be blamed on the wayward walk
your mother, father took, just as much as on your own fist:
When I see you suffer, I will point to their fat hands.

Because someone else will punish you, so I don't have to
do anything but feel wretched as a horse's head
for you, poor sweet sucker—lonely-sentence you.

Because even if you have fucked up,
fallen short, slipshod, blotched,
blundered backwards, clangored like cast iron,
gone south and gone all-the-way bad—

just because you are beautiful, for you
three times I touch my head to the ground.

The Poet and Her True Love

He said: If you were my wife I'd beat you.
She said: If I was your wife I would divorce you.

He said: If you tried to divorce me—you would get *two* beatings a day.
She said: If you ever beat me, I'd kill you.

He said: Now it's three. Three beatings a day.
She said: I'd tear one of your ears off.

He said: That's it. The backhand on the weekend, the belt during the week.
She said: I will never marry you.

He said: We will grow old together.
She said: I'll push your wheelchair down the staircase.

He said: You'll get fat and sleep in my bed.
She said: I'll burn the bed.

He said: You'll be just like your mother.
She said: (pause) Don't you ever again say such a thing.

He said: You'll wash my flannel shirts.
She said: In the toilet.

He said: You'll cut my hair twice a month.
She said: With a handsaw.

He said: We will be dogs together.
She said: Yeah. Wild dogs. Mad dogs. Killer dogs.

He said: No. Love dogs.

Fairy Tale

Why, there they are both, baked in that pie...
—Titus Andronicus

    In a fairy tale, three men break into a home, tie up
a sleeping family and cover their mouths with dull
silver tape. One man says, *I'll hold Mother by the wrists,*
so she can watch, as the other two scissor off
her six-year-old daughter's nightgown. They bend her
over a folding chair and stab a wooden spoon
into the eyelet between her legs.
    In a fairy tale, a mother is ferocious. She tears her body
away from her arms. The first man is left holding
her bloody elbows, her two hands that flap like fish.
She doesn't need them anyway. She uses teeth for the rescue.
    In a fairy tale, the men are cut up and cooked into a meat so rich
that swallowing a spoonful is enough
to grow a mother new limbs from her dress sleeves, like starfish do.

My Funny Valentine

for Hsiao Hui Tan

"He gets very angry with me," she said. "He is so violent
with his love. And jealous. Of everything. If I make fried
rice for the African man at our deli, or if I talk to someone
for too long at the gym. He yells like an animal and his face
looks like fire. If I spend too much time with his mother,
or especially if my skirt is too short—he throws all sorts
of utensils at the bedroom wall—says I'm going to drive him
to drink again. He says his other girlfriends never gave him
so much trouble—not even the ones who were tall and had
silicone titties—and all I ever wonder is, what it will be like
when he stops loving me. And he will. Just like that.
This is how it happens: After punching a fist like a sledgehammer
into the wall and kicking down a door and throwing dinner out
the window onto the street—then crying and saying forgive me,
forgive me, forgive me and kissing your whole face as if
there is a fever that makes him do it—and you think only
the most powerful kind of funky never-ending deep-metal love
could make a man behave this way—then just like that,
he stops. And all I ever wonder is, what that will be like."

The Poet and the Truck Driver

She said: So. The road is all yours now.
He said: It's an artery not much different than a river.
She said: That tractor trailer is like the mountain you always wanted.
He said: Well, second gear sticks a little.

She said: Gas leaks are like pools of kaleidoscopes.
He said: The highway gets inky at night.
She said: Some days, I don't speak to anyone.
He said: Read to me.

She said: No. You never cared much for blank verse.
He said: Afternoons I sing Sinatra over the CB.
She said: Why don't you leave her for me?
He said: Because I see the shape of her in sunup.

She said: We'd have hated each other anyway.
He said: But we'd have loved other things.

She said: I love the double yellow lines.
He said: I love the blue feathered quill.

She said: Well then. The road is all yours now.
He said: Glitter still gets to me. Every red reflector reminds me of you.

The Art of Compromise

A couple is in love in every way, except for the way they kiss.

He prefers one kiss per day, either on her pillow, just after sunrise,
or right before midnight, next to his window, under the moon.

She prefers one hundred kisses per day. Over the kitchen sink,
the arm of the couch, the headboard, the toilet; inside the bathtub,
the closet, the elevator; in front of the neighbors, the mailman,
a police officer, his dog; upside-down, against a tree trunk, in roller-
skates or while wearing a gorilla's head for a hat.

For the first year of their love she decides to give in. To let him be the man
he has always been. But after six kiss-less months, her mouth goes bone dry.
When she poses in the mirror she can't remember how to pucker or pout.
She gives up chewing gum and lip gloss. Her tongue begins to shrink.

Because he loves her, he notices her misery.

For the second year of their love, he decides to give in. To let her be the woman
she has always been. But after six kiss-happy months, he has developed a habit
of drooling. His beard and his bowties are stained and sticky.
He gives up coffee and onions. His two favorite treats.

Because she loves him, she notices his misery.

For the third year of their love, neither of them are able to sleep a wink.
They stay up all night pacing the left and right sides of the bed, trying
to come up with a solution. Every now and then he leaps over the mattress
and plunges toward her, pointing his kiss at her like a gun. She ducks
and dodges with all her might, clams her face shut with a hair pin.

On the first day of the fourth year of their love they are both worn out
from the year-long insomnia. They collapse into each other's arms and snore
loudly for seven days. On the eighth day, he awakens her with his mouth.
Their lips are swollen like plums from fatigue and heartache and his kiss is fatter
and deeper than fifty kisses. Her tongue curls back into her mouth like a happy snake
who has just been fed a horse for dinner. There's a hiss inside her. She is filled silly.

The Poet and the Egyptian

He said: I remember your name and the way you smell.
She said: I waited and waited for you to send a message.

He said: I can never forget your sexy lips, your beautiful nose,
       your small breasts.
She said: I don't think you wrote a book after all.

He said: Tell me why I hate you.
She said: Do you still sell shoes?

He said: Tell me why I talk about you to the nun who raised me.
She said: What does she say?

He said: Nevermind. Tell me if you look more like your mother or your father.
She said: I look most like a certain kind of bird.

He said: You like the left side of your face more than the right.
She said: You're drunk.

He said: These are not really pictures of you.
She said: I remember posing.

He said: You don't hold your arm in this way.
She said: I can lift my leg over my head when I swim.

He said: When I dream of you, your skin is like sand.
She said: Are there cornflowers in the desert?

He said: I want to memorize your fingernails.
She said: Are mirages always blue?

He said: I love your small breasts.
She said: Does everyone in Egypt have eyes like the tip of a paintbrush?

He said: I can spell your name in Arabic.
She said: Write it here. With glue.

Bangladesh

Everything was different in Bangladesh. The distance
between two men, the flavor of milk, the color green.
Here, they think their city *crowded*—but the R train
to Queens almost always allows me a seat. At the restaurant
where I work, the waitresses wear lips like fat red prawns.
They call me, *Sweetie*, even though they hardly know me
and cannot see how strange it is for me when they chant
Goodnight, embrace me with their bare arms and stamp
their mouths to my cheek. Yet, they have heard of Ramadan,
know I am fasting until sundown, because it is repeated again
and again in their news. They think nothing of the couple
in the booth, his hand under her skirt, her tongue inside his ear.
How romantic, they say, when I tell them I went against
my family's wishes, chose my own bride, filled her belly with fruit,
and brought her to America. *That's a real man*, one whispers,
as another asks the meaning of my son's name, and I tell her, *Water*.

Hip-Hop in the Desert

My name is Mohamed Zahid, he says, and bows,
his fresh white kandoora sailing at his back
like a ghost that follows him into the dune field.
He tells us it's time to go, and I lean in to the camel
I've been sitting with, take one last photo of her
pointed eyes. We climb into the SUV, turn on the GPS
to nowhere, and drive into a plantation of soft pyramids.
He barrels straight up a slipface of red dirt as one thousand
tiny avalanches take the roller-coaster freefall with us.
There is nothing left or right for miles except for these hills
that seem to fold into giant fortune cookies, soft as talcum,
and the wheels dig into the dune's sharp crest faster and
faster—and now, we are all gasps and hiccups—and Mohamed
Zahid reaches one giant thumb toward the stereo.
He turns off the sacred music that has been luring us
into the desert—suddenly there are no more piping lutes,
no cymbals—no peal of sad-woman moaning—instead, hard
candy begins to knock from deep inside the speakers—
hand-clapping breakbeats that tick and stutter—drum loops,
and every mouthful of American profanity that has ever been
invented. I wonder if he knows what they are saying, or if
he just likes the way a man's voice punches out poetry
like a factory machine. In the rearview mirror, I see his
moustache, which is the same shape as the Arabic symbols
on a stop sign, gently bobbing up and down to a 1, 2 count.
I imagine him taking this rap music home to his wife,
playing it for her after they are inside their house, after
she takes off her abaya. I wonder if she likes it, too. And if so,
does he let her dance? Or does she just roll her eyes far back
into her forehead, as he plays the hook.

Holy Is the Secular World

HOLY is a world where the unwed can sex the Three Jewels
with the Flaming Chalice of the mouth.

HAIL a place where the Hand of Fatima
can enter the Endless Knot of the Triple Goddess
and a man can kiss another man's Peace Pipe without shame.

BLESSED is the Rose who wears her Bindi
when she caresses her own Crescent—

PRAISE to the Medicine Wheel
for washing away a child.

SALVATION is the indulgence of divorce.

PRAYER is the purr the body makes when it dances.

RITUAL is the construction of arms and legs in love-making—
      their Swastika shape on the mattress.

SACRED is a woman who is allowed to swim.
SACRED is the horsepower of lipstick.
SACRED is the muscle of whiskey and wine.
SACRED is a man's hands.
SACRED is a man's hands.
SACRED is the girl who gets pregnant at seventeen—
      let them call her a sinner or say she ruined her life—
SACRED is her daughter's eyes like sharp blackbirds.

DIVINE are the backbones of the dragons that lived before us.

HOLY is the secular world:

the Witchcraft of asymmetry
that brought us to Ecstasy
with one big bang.

When I fell in love with the leper

he took me to his colony.
We went to the Quiet Island
by rowboat, entered the city

through a stone gate. We walked
down the Street of Pain, along
the coast that kissed the Sea

of Crete. He led me under palm trees,
inside cloth shops and an empty castle.
One girl liked to sing from a wooden balcony.

Some of the other lepers were married,
lived together in small houses,
with a garden outside to tend, a few hens,

a dog or cats. It happened there that lepers,
just like other people, fell in love.

5. The Silk Shop

The String

It was a Saturday afternoon in spring. I was teaching a poetry workshop. I gave my students ten minutes to scratch into the skins of their notebooks, and as I waited, I noticed a hole in the wall with one single string coming out of it.

Stop writing, I said, and pointed toward the hole and the string. Their faces looked small as bats.

I'm going to pull it, I warned them, and reached for it with my tiny fist. I pulled it past seven desks, past the trash can, out the door.

When I reached the hallway, I called back to them: *Class is cancelled. I need to know how far this string will go.*

I pulled the string down five flights of stairs, past the security guard and along the grey stone of Astor Place. There was an Indian man selling incense on the corner; I pulled the string through a cloud of smoke.

I pulled the string down Broadway, through a street fair with fresh watermelon in Styrofoam cups and funnel cakes with drizzled chocolate that looked like lace.

I pulled the string through Chinatown, past the pageant of green Buddhas, purple silk, gold chains, and pastries in the shape of lungs.

When I yanked it across Wall Street a man in a black square suit yelled: *Get out of my way!* A homeless woman with a polka-dot headscarf whispered: *Never give up, Girl.*

I pulled the string across the Brooklyn Bridge. I could have sworn diamonds were growing from that river. Cars honked at me with horns that sounded like gorillas and I held the string up high in the air for them as if it were a trophy.

My mother called on my cell phone as I was pulling the string down Atlantic Avenue. *I can't talk now*, I told her, *I need to know how far this string will go.*

I pulled the string inside Greenwood Cemetery, over the headstones of Bill the Butcher and Basquiat. Then I pulled the string along Fort Hamilton Parkway.

Mack trucks boomed at my side. One or two slowed down to catcall.

I turned onto a street I used to know (*one block south of the movie theater, and cattycorner to the funeral home*).

Suddenly, the string jerked me to a stop. I pulled and heaved until it tore cuts into my hands. But it would not budge.

When I looked up, you were standing in front of me. *I've been waiting*, you said.

I let the string fall to the sidewalk, and put a knuckle to your lips for you to kiss. And as you did, you whispered three things: *damn. sweet. good.*

Doppelganger Love Poem

after Arundhati Roy

In the book, one twin knows the other is at the door,
even before he knocks. They sleep with their arms and legs
intertwined like sausages. You cannot blame them for this worship.
How blessed, to embrace your very own rib, shoulder and throat.
Those of us without a second self take lovers, and suspect they are
a portion of ourselves, just because they fit into us like a shoelace.
We think they will know we are at the door, even before we knock.
Some nights, I know what my lover is going to say in his sleep,
even before he says it. He unties my braids in the dark, with only
one hand. If the swimming discs in his eyes were candies, I know
what that flavor would taste like. At times, I am too full-color
for his tooth, too bold in flesh and frenzy. I know this. We try
to locate the handprints we leave in each other's strange clay
that, most days, we are too reckless to notice.

He said, you are a white elephant,

always drinking tiger-milk, then spitting it
on cowboys to get attention. Your nose
keeps getting longer! You wrinkled up

the left side of your face to make me fall for you,
and so, you were it—the apple and the light,
the turtle and the bird. I tied myself to you

like a boat dock. I saved up pennies
to buy small red fish and blue glass bottles.
I tried to make the old hat last—but it split

apart like jacket snaps, rotted away like that old brown
rattletrap you used to drive. Now all I have left
is a gut-bucket full of all the things we made together:

five ropes of braided licorice,
three sets of seashell wind chimes
and a bird's nest of the wiry hairs

that we tore off the coconut we broke
on your mother's kitchen floor,
that muddy summer, ten years ago.

Trading Pigs for Love

1.

Dear Love:

I don't know why it is you don't believe
I love you.

If you want me to, I'll cut off one of my toes
in exchange for your love.

I can use a hacksaw and let *you* pick
which little piggy will go.

I'll be waiting for you
in the bedroom
with my tool belt.

2.

Line up the things I hate most in the world
and dare me to swallow them, to prove how much
I love you.

A blended rat milkshake.
A fistful of mayonnaise.
The heart of my dead dog.

Blindfold me and give me a paper bag filled with one hundred thumbs.
I'll know which one is yours.

3.

I love you so much that some nights
I wish for a terrible accident, gray glass
littering the road, and you, paralyzed
from hipbone on down.

Then:

        No one wants you anymore. But me.
        I clunk into your blue hospital and against the wind
        push your wheelchair uphill all the way home.

        You jerk a little from spinal shock and nerve loss,
        but I've got strong arms so the trip is easy.

        Your legs are like branches dragging
        and I am bright yellow with joy—

        I got you now.
        You cannot tell me this
        isn't love.

        And even if, on some mornings, a creak in the floor
        whispers: *Leave Her. Leave Her—*
        it won't matter—
        your legs
        do not work
        anyway.

Love in an Ice Cream Truck

Yesterday, I took a walk downtown. It was winter
everywhere, except for the inside of my mouth.
I saw an ice cream truck parked on 3rd Avenue.
The man inside drew me toward his window
with a whistle that reminded me of the noise
a peacock makes. He had good-looking lips,
which always gets to me, so I gave him an attitude,
"Who the hell's gonna buy ice cream on a day
like today?" He didn't say a word, but instead,
winked, opened the side door, kicked out a two-step
ladder and whispered, "Come in."

Inside, everything was made of chrome. Rows
of waffle cones hung from the ceiling like Chinese
lanterns. He pulled a sheet of brown paper
from a large roll and laid it on the floor. When I took
off his shirt, he had a tattoo of a racecar on his torso.
"Zoom, zoom," I said, and we started making love.
He held my face in his hands as if it were a grapefruit
he was testing for ripeness, and he barely breathed.

When we stopped, the only noise was the purr
of a refrigerator. "There's a man you love,
isn't there?" he asked me.
"There is."
"What does he do wrong, that made you
end up in here with me?"
"He doesn't kiss me enough," I said.
"Why don't you leave him?"
"Because I like the way he sleeps.
And I like that he never prays."

The moon crept into the truck like a thief.
"I have to go."
He kissed me nine times from soda fountain to doorstep.
When I was almost a block away, he stuck his head
out the ice cream window and yelled: "Have you ever

seen a volcano?" I didn't even look back. As I followed the sidewalk south I heard his voice three more times:
"You are a volcano! You are a volcano! You are a volcano!"

The Smallest Bird on Earth

What is the smallest bird on earth? he asks, and she doesn't answer.
The fan is humming like an old machine. That afternoon,
at the Wayne County Fair, the Blue Ribbon Bantam was for sale
for only six dollars. On the ride home to Brooklyn, they started
fighting. She tried to get out of the car at a stoplight. Later, he left
the bed four times to sleep on the couch. She swore she'd change
her number, they'd never speak again. The fan kept humming like
an old machine, and soon they were kissing. How do they make love
so golden, after a cyclone of curses? When they finish, they are so sorry
that their bodies drip over one another like honey. He tells her how
yesterday, he saw a dead body on the street, a woman hit by a truck.
They covered her face with a white sheet. The fan is humming like
an old machine. *What is the smallest bird on earth?* he asks, and she says,
hummingbird. blue hummingbird.

Twenty-Four Hours

You are cooking catfish in the kitchen and I notice
a tree branch outside the bedroom has positioned itself
into the letter K. Like always, you never speak
while you eat. After dinner, you tear sugarcane
apart with your teeth. When we lie down together,
I knead my fingers into the thick skin on your back.
You tell me the bottoms of my feet feel like banana peels.
I tell you I know where the saltiest parts of your body are:
under here, *right there*, and *this*, *this*. Sometimes,
we make love with mosquitoes, because you left
a window open. They feel like tiny vampires. It is
a different kind of kiss. When we sleep, I hold on tight,
as if I'm carrying you into a river of bedsheets.
As we dive into the deep part, I wonder if you are ever sad.
If you will ever need anyone. Just after two, I get up
to use the toilet. You wake and think I've left,
until you see my panties next to the pillow and my
earrings on the nightstand. When I get back
to the bed, I find you waiting for me. *Don't ever
do that again*, you say, *Next time, leave a note*.
Before I'm under the blanket, you're snoring.
In the morning, you tell me you dreamt of flying.
But not too high. Only about eight feet off the ground,
and very slow. In the park, we pass a white-haired woman
on a bicycle. *Look*, you point to her, *See what a pretty
old lady she is. That's how you will be*. We stop at the corner
to buy an onion. The grapes are a terrific black-like color.
You tell me that once, before your mother died,
you caught her watching you, as you washed
a bowl of grapes with salt water. That she looked as if
she could not believe you came from her. In the elevator,
I wonder if you ever catch me watching you, if I look as if
I have no idea who you are, even though I've slept
naked with you for more than a hundred nights. You drip oil
into a pan and put it on the stove to fry. You are cooking catfish
in the kitchen and I notice a tree branch outside the bedroom
has positioned itself into the letter K. The oil makes snake

79

sounds. Heat is gushing from the radiator at my feet, saying:
shhhhh, shhhhh. Your guitar is lying on the couch
like a tired woman. You call to me: *My girl, come eat.
Before it gets cold. Come eat, come eat.*

The last time they made love

she wore black knee-socks to cover up the burns
on her legs. It was just before Christmas, and the radiator
was pumping heat like a steamboat.

They pulled the mattress off its frame, slapped it
to the hardwood floor. She took the flower from her hair,
hid it under the pillow, used her lace panties to rub the lipstick
off of her face—and once he fell asleep, she spent the night

braiding the tiny gold hairs on his chest
into the shape of a potholder—knotting and twisting
and knotting him up—to make sure that in the morning

there'd be a keepsake of how small her fingers were,
so that when she was gone for good, he'd remember
how the palm of her hand
was only as big as an ear.

The Snake Who Swallows His Own Tail

What if this is the only thing
we can get right? The way I wrap
my two legs like a double helix
around one of yours, weave my arm
to orbit your neck, plant three
fingernails in a shoulder blade.
The way you wear the place between
my breasts like a sleeping mask,
jungle your hands through
the web we make of skin and hair.
Then, the way you feed on my mouth,
like the snake who swallows
his own tail. You say, *I think I'm on fire*,
and the only way to extinguish the flame
is to undress and stretch over me
like a red iron. I say, *I think there are
jumping beans in my pillow*, I hear them
whisper in Spanish each time our lips
bracket. We don't dare go outside today.
We know the street I live on
will make us talk about why
this has to end. You sleep hard
on my chest and I try to think up
a silken cord to run from your forehead
to mine, or a stone circle to gate the bed,
so we can stay inside
this box spring's bony frame,
from now until the sun burns out.

The Eye Is an Organ of Light

When we first met, we each wore the imprint of a cup and saucer
inside our palm. There were sixteen kidneys of light I saw you in.
Five of them were neon.

In time, I memorized the rainbow of plaids in your wardrobe,
the acute angles of the alphabet on your body,
and every word you ever wrote.

Then, I went to Africa. Met a man who fell asleep on a beach
with his wife in his arms, and woke up holding a tree trunk.
He found a different part of her under each of the branches.
A pelican had stolen her hair.

I came home. You'd gotten a tattoo of another woman's lips
behind your right ear. When I saw its popcorn-shape,
it felt as if there was a planet between my lungs, instead of a fist.

I packed all your shirts in a paper bag. Considered making a tin-can
telephone, with a string as long as Brooklyn, to call you on
to ask why you did it. But I already knew what you would say:

Her body was a witch. I could not help myself.

Where the Good Men Live

Just for today, I don't want to write
about the flaws of men.
I want to write about
their incomparable
beauty, the way I adore
every angle
of their hands,
the boat-like shape
of their torsos,
the animal
that lives
in their arms.
Today, I want to say:
I'm certain
the jelly-like thing
that rests behind
your forehead
is sadness.
I think I can take it out
with my mouth.
Today, I want to write:
You are better
than cherries.
By the time I finish typing
I'll have fashioned
exquisite statues
out of regular men.
Then I'll turn
on the news,
or I'll turn
the page
of some newsprint,
or I'll turn
in my bed
and the things
I'll see men do
will not be fit for poetry.

At least not this kind
of poetry, the kind that praises
their muscle and blesses
the stars that steer them.
This poem is not about
the inability to forgive.
It's about wanting
to find an island
where the good men live,
wanting to take a boat there
and arrive with flags
and flowers
in a kaleidoscope
of colors,
wanting to embrace them
like a straitjacket
and only let go
for long enough
to write a poem
or two
painting men
as bright heroes
because on this island
they are.

The Animal of Love

And once they had finished, they went limp,
boneless, chin in an armpit, tongue in hair,
arm dangling from the bedpost, leg bent
as a boomerang. Where had they gone together?
Where words could not fly?
If they had been birds, there'd have been a mess
of feathers in the bedroom. If they had been
zebras, black x's would mark the sheets.
If they had been dolphins, they'd've spoken
sonic language while making love, ultrasounds that said:
> *I will swim belly-to-belly*
> *with you forever, and if you die first,*
> *I will beach myself, because it would be*
> *too lonely to live without your silver flesh.*

Acknowledgments and Thanks

Grateful acknowledgment is made to the editors of the following publications where these poems first appeared:

Dorado: "Blessing," "The last time they made love"
Ekleksographia: "Biracial Marriage," "The Secret Language of Symbols"
Hanging Loose: "Dialect of a Skirt," "Lucky Bee," "Socks and Swimsuits"
Mipoesias: "In Jacklight," "Mannequins at Lunch"
Mustachioed: "He said, You are a white elephant"
New York Quarterly: "The Poet and the Truck Driver"
OCHO #6: "Corpse Dream," "Fishwife," "Marilyn and the Spelling Bee"
Sink Review: "Pocket Wife"
Sixth Finch: "The Waitress"
Spindle: "Stealing the Baby"
Spoon River Poetry Review: "The Word-Lover's Miscarriage"
Texas Review: "The Third Miscarriage of Marilyn Monroe," "The Smallest Bird on Earth"
Trespass Magazine: "The Poet and the Egyptian"
30/30: "The Art of Compromise," "Grandmother Love Poem"

A live recording of "The First Plastic Surgery Patient on Earth" first appeared on the website *Indiefeed.com*.

Immeasurable thanks to the poets, figures, mentors, students and friends who have supported and inspired this book directly or indirectly:

Sharon Mesmer, Bob Holman, Rachel McKibbens, Roger Bonair-Agard, David Lehman, Patricia Smith, Willie Perdomo, Tara Betts, April Jones, Aricka Foreman, Queen GodIs, Mahogany Brown, MC K-Swift, Shaun "Scheme" Redwood, Maureen Meade, Tahani Salah, Kesed Ragin, Jamila Lyiscott, Giselle Buchanan, Kiara Towns, Katie and Laura Medico, Anne Walters, Jonathan "Good-for-Nothing" Gabrielson, Nick Ogozarek, Jonathan Keith, Alex Valiente, Bobby Gonzales, Grant Kretchik, Jason Napolsky, Amy Rilling, and the Roder Family.

Hanging Loose Press: Bob Hershon, Donna Brook, Marie Carter, and especially my meticulous and ever-patient editor, Dick Lourie. Michael Cirelli, for his endless support in making this book happen.

Olivia Seally, for making the book so beautiful.
Linda Turley, for making ME *and* the book so beautiful.
Black Cracker, for making the book become a real, fabulous, visual piece of art.
Dave Johnson, for everything. Everything.
Jeffrey Arbeeny, my muse. I might never have become a poet without you.
Ohene Bonsu, for loyalty.
Hsiao Hui Tan, my muse. And my heart.
Kunal Vora, for the way you believe in me.
Robin Andre, for love, love, love. And also for love, love, love.

Anne and Gene Miller, for teaching me what true love is.
My grandfather.
My ever-loving mother and father, for being so hard on me. For making me work for it.
My best friend in the world, my brother.